MEMORY LANE
AYLESBURY
THE POST-WAR YEARS

MEMORY LANE
AYLESBURY

THE POST-WAR YEARS

Photographs from the archives of **The Bucks Herald**

breedon books
PUBLISHING

First published in Great Britain in 2001 by
The Breedon Books Publishing Company Limited
Breedon House, 3 The Parker Centre, Derby, DE21 4SZ.

To purchase copies of photographs in this book
please contact
The Bucks Herald and Advertiser,
2-4 Exchange Street, Aylesbury, Bucks, HP20 1UJ.
Telephone: 01296 318300

ISBN 1 85983 263 6

Printed and bound by Butler & Tanner, Frome, Somerset
Jacket printing by GreenShires Ltd, Leicester

Contents

Introduction

WALK in to the newspaper file room of *The Bucks Herald* and its sister paper *The Bucks Advertiser* – forgetting about more modern ways of sifting through files on-screen – and simply lift down one of the hefty volumes from the shelves, turn the ageing pages and enjoy the experience of re-living things as they happened day-by-day, week-by-week.

That is what this book is all about… a glimpse of Aylesbury and the surrounding area as it was in the post war years up to the late 1960s.

All the pictures used have come from the archives of both newspapers which have been a part of the local community since the mid-1800s.

And while there is no way in which a book such as this can paint a comprehensive picture of 'the way things were', it can – and we hope does – give a flavour of life and events in and around Aylesbury which have been caught on camera.

Here thanks are owed to local press photographers such as the late Alex Weston, chief photographer of *The Bucks Advertiser* for many years, who was among those – including also Maurice Cousins of *The Bucks Herald*, Roy Palmer, *Herald/Advertiser* photographer, both now retired from the papers, and Barry Keen – who have done so much to provide us with a permanent record of the many aspects of life in the Vale over this period.

Local newspaper photographers, past and present, the journalists and the newspapers themselves, have made – and continue to make – an invaluable contribution to preserving the community history of an area, something in which both *The Bucks Herald* and *The Bucks Advertiser* take great pride.

But such records can remain 'on file', gathering dust, if it were not for books such as this.

It was never intended that it should give a complete picture of life during nearly three decades but rather that it should be a fond look back, within a time scale that many can remember, at a town and district which in recent years has witnessed many dramatic changes.

There are well over 300 photographs reproduced in the following pages which, put together, give, we believe, an invaluable insight in to local life.

In so many ways each picture tells its own story.

We have included captions which, while every care has been taken to ensure accuracy, were never intended to tell the whole story but simply to inform, and in some instances remind, people of what was happening in those post war years and the 'Swinging Sixties'.

We hope readers will enjoy it and for many this book will bring back happy memories.

Of course much has happened in Aylesbury and The Vale since these photographs were taken.

But that is another story…

The smile says it all! The Queen opens the Stoke Mandeville Stadium in August 1969 – a date which coincided with the 21st anniversary of the staging of the first international paraplegic games. During her hour long visit The Queen toured the stadium, accompanied by Sir Ludwig Guttmann (pictured immediately right of The Queen), founder of the Stoke Mandeville Games and president of the International Stoke Mandeville Games Committee, and unveiled a plaque to mark the occasion.

Crowned Heads and Coronations

Outside the stadium The Queen walked among the crowds and met many of those who had helped raise around £300,000 to pay for equipping and building the stadium, the brainchild of Sir Ludwig who was convinced that sport could give the disabled the incentive they needed to come to terms with their disability.

Crowds lined Kingsbury, Buckingham Street and the High Street for a previous visit in April 1962 to see the Queen. But for many the gathering point was in the Market Square where row upon row of Sea Cadets, Army Cadets, members of the Air Training Corps, Boy Scouts and Girl Guides stood shoulder-to-shoulder with more than 100 apprentices from RAF Halton who formed a guard of honour.

Thousands of Aylesbury residents turned out on 6 April 1962 to welcome The Queen to the town, having accepted an invitation to see the work which was being done by the then Aylesbury Borough Council to provide council homes and also to look at plans for the re-development of the town centre.

At the new housing estate in Oxford Road, Aylesbury, The Queen was welcomed to the town by the Mayor, Cllr Maurice Buckingham and, before touring some of the new homes, was shown models of the different types of houses being built in the Borough as well as a model of the planned changes for the town centre. The Queen visited two of the council houses – No.142, home of Mr and Mrs Powell and their two daughters and their neighbours at No. 140, home of Mr and Mrs Coyde and their son and daughter.

After her drive through the town she was entertained to lunch at The Grange School – a lunch which had originally been planned to take place at the Town Hall but which, a few weeks earlier, had been seriously damaged by fire. Over 200 guests were invited and sat down to a meal which included Aylesbury duck!

In July 1952 The Queen came to Halton to present her Colour to the No.1 School of Technical Training, making Halton the first establishment of its kind to receive such an honour. The visit also marked the passing out of the 63rd entry of aircraft apprentices and the first entry of apprentices from Pakistan. In total 1,700 RAF apprentices took part in the event which included an inspection by The Queen.

It was July 1959 that the Princess Royal attended a garden party organised by the Bucks WVS in the grounds of Waddesdon Manor as part of the voluntary service 21st anniversary and inspected more than 200 members.

Built at a cost of £127,367, the Aylesbury High School in Walton Road was officially opened by Princess Alexandra in May 1960... a rainy afternoon which meant that one pupil was chosen for a very special duty, to escort the Princess in to the building under cover of an umbrella.

Marking the centenary of the Bucks Constabulary in May 1957 – described in the press as being 'their proudest day' – the Duchess of Kent visited RAF Halton to inspect more than 600 police officers. They included dog handlers, members of the women's police division, special constables, two police motorcyclists, 10 traffic patrol cars and personnel manning a police van. The Princess, speaking from a flower decked dais on either side of which were top-hatted constables dressed in the uniform of the constabulary 100 years ago, said the county should take great pride in all those associated with the police force.

Vice-Admiral Earl Mountbatten of Burma visited RAF Halton on 8 May 1951 for the passing out of the 59th Entry of aircraft apprentices after their three years training and praised former apprentices for their contribution towards the defeat of the Japanese in Burma.

Crowds lined the entrance to The Grange School, Aylesbury on 20 June 1959 to catch a glimpse of the Duchess of Kent when she arrived to open the 10th anniversary and rally dealing with health education organised by Mothers' Clubs and child welfare centres in Bucks.

Also during her visit to the area the Duchess of Kent opened the new admission unit – Beacon House – at St John's Hospital, Stone which had been built at a cost of £150,000 and, accompanied by Sir George Schuster, chairman of the Oxford Regional Health Authority, reviewed a guard of honour of nurses from the hospital.

Members of the Bucks St John Ambulance Brigade were in Aylesbury town centre on 31 May 1957 to take part in a parade at which the salute was taken by Countess Mountbatten of Burma.

Attending the parade of the Bucks St John Ambulance Brigade in Aylesbury in May 1957, their Commander in Chief, the Countess Mountbatten of Burma, shook hands with every one of the 1,660 members of the brigade who attended… and thanked the local Press photographers for the 'unobtrusive way' they had done their work.

Flags of 27 nations flew in the grounds of Stoke Mandeville Hospital in August 1957 representing the countries taking part in the 10th annual and sixth international sports festival for the paralysed – the Stoke Mandeville Games – attended by the Duchess of Gloucester who opened the two days of sport and was welcomed by a guard of honour made up of competitors. To the right of the picture is Sir Ludwig Guttmann, founder of the games.

Just some of the crowds which gathered in Aylesbury on Remembrance Sunday, 1951 for a visit by the Duchess of Kent who unveiled a memorial tablet in St Mary's Parish Church in memory of the officers and men of the Buckinghamshire Light Infantry who gave their lives in World War Two.

When the Duchess of Kent visited Aylesbury to unveil a memorial tablet in the parish church to recognise the sacrifice of officers and men in World War Two, the service was attended by 95 relatives of the 117 men known to have died while serving with the Buckinghamshire Light Infantry.

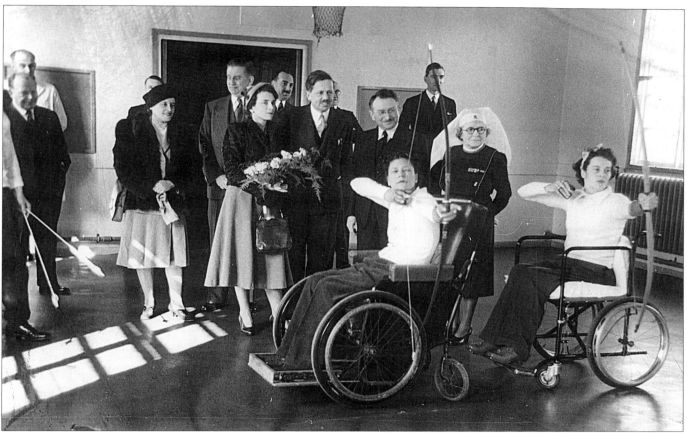

It was a chance for the Duchess of Gloucester to watch paraplegics at Stoke Mandeville Hospital testing their archery skills when she paid an informal visit there in March 1949, accompanied by the Minister of Pensions, the Hon A.H. Marquand.

They began with just a handful of employees in Aylesbury. But printers and bookbinders Hazell Watson & Viney – who, when our picture was taken, had premises in Tring Road and Bicester Road – grew to become the largest employer in the town. Just before World War Two they employed 1,600 people, approximately a third of the population of the town and in June 1958, the Duke of Edinburgh visited their factories.

Friday the 13th might be unlucky for some, but not for thousands of Aylesbury people on that day in June 1958. Many managed to catch a glimpse of the Duke of Edinburgh – while others were able to meet and chat to him – when he spent most of the day in the town, visiting local industry, opening Quarrendon school and, at the end of the day, calling in at Stoke Mandeville Hospital. 'He was due to leave at 4.30pm but the departure time had to be put back as he was too interested and did not want to leave,' it was reported.

June 1958 and hundreds of schoolchildren line the streets waiting for the Duke of Edinburgh.

Having piloted himself in a Royal Navy helicopter from Buckingham Palace, the Duke of Edinburgh arrived in Aylesbury on 13 June 1958 and, during a day spent in the town, attended the opening of Quarrendon Secondary School where he unveiled a plaque.

A tour of Bucks in October 1952 by the Duke of Edinburgh as part of Bucks Playing Fields Week, took the royal visitor to Cuddington where he met local scouts and planted a tree to commemorate his visit. The Duke of Edinburgh also had lunch at The Bulls Head in Market Square, Aylesbury – now the site of the Hale Leys shopping centre – where he was welcomed on the cobbled forecourt by the Lord Lieutenant, Lord Cottesloe.

They turned out in their thousands in Aylesbury and other towns and villages in Bucks when the Duke of Edinburgh made a whistle stop tour of the county – travelling more than 70 miles in six hours and shaking hundreds of hands. His visit, on Tuesday, 14 October 1952, was to mark Bucks Playing Fields Week which had been organised by the Buckinghamshire Playing Fields Association.

More than 3,000 spectators turned up at the Alfred Rose Park for the Aylesbury Coronation Sports in May 1953 when the shock of the day was provided by champion athlete Mcdonald Bailey who finished a poor third in the 100 yards race and blamed a sluggish start on the fact his legs had tightened up during his car journey from London. First home was teenager M.J. Ruddy.

Led by an impressive white Shire horse, this cart, carrying the 'Queen' of the village, Heather Francis, accompanied by local children, headed the procession through the village of Kingswood in 1953 to mark the Coronation.

As part of the Coronation celebrations in June 1953 five couples competed in the Aylesbury Duck Trials which were held in the shadow of the clock tower in Market Square and during which they had to reveal their marital secrets to a crowd of over 200. And what else should the first prize be but a plump Aylesbury duck!

On 22 May 1953 children from Tring Road School, Aylesbury, went home from the school's fifth anniversary party clutching their souvenir Coronation mugs which had been presented to them by the local education committee.

Crowds, including a large number of children, gathered in the Market Square, Aylesbury, on a chilly February morning in 1952 to listen as the High Sheriff of Buckinghamshire announced the accession of a new sovereign – Her Majesty Queen Elizabeth II.

Market Square, Aylesbury,
1952 as the High Sheriff of
Buckinghamshire announced
the accession of a new
sovereign – Her Majesty
Queen Elizabeth II

As part of the Coronation celebrations, residents in Eaton Road, Aylesbury were determined to enjoy themselves and, no matter what age you were, you were welcome to the celebrations.

Instead of a street party, why not get out 'to the great outdoors?' That is just what residents of Middle Road in Aylesbury did when they organised their Coronation party, held in a field close to their homes.

This was the scene – the picture being taken high above the Market Square, Aylesbury, in June 1953 – as the town joined in the national Coronation celebrations with a procession of decorated floats.

Attending a street party in Abbey Road, Aylesbury in June 1953 to celebrate the Coronation were these delightful characters – the Carrington triplets, Jeremy, Paul and Simon – who were dressed in miniature versions of the uniforms of the army, navy and airforce 'as proud soldiers of The Queen', it was reported.

They were distributed in their thousands. This little lad is almost lost among the Coronation mugs which were waiting in Aylesbury Town Hall in June 1953 to be distributed to local children.

As part of the June 1953 Coronation celebrations a bathing beauty contest was held in Aylesbury and, while it is obvious the judges had a difficult task, they eventually decided to award the title to Miss Daphne Bennet – and the expression on her face tells its own story!

The British Legion in Aylesbury marked the Coronation by organising their own beauty competition and here the winner, Miss Edna Williams, accompanied by her attendants, is seen being driven around the Molefields estate on the outskirts of the town – an estate of prefabricated buildings which was created at the start of World War Two to accommodate 'refugees' from other parts of the country which it was known would suffer heavy bombing.

Named after royalty, it was open house in Victoria Street and Albert Street, Aylesbury, as residents took part in the Coronation celebrations with a tea party in the middle of the road and a huge Coronation cake in the middle of the table. 'Lemonade was flowing and residents and neighbours were full of good spirit', we reported.

Fancy dress was very much the order of the day when those living in Ardenham Street and West Street, Aylesbury, joined forces for their own Coronation street party.

Our photographer did not have to try very hard to get this group to 'smile for the camera', they were obviously enjoying their Coronation party held at the Southcourt scout hut in June 1953.

They were out in force at Halton fo join in the celebrations to mark the accession of Queen Elizabeth.

As a 'starter' to their Coronation tea, the children of Cottesloe Road on the Southcourt estate in Aylesbury took part in a fancy dress parade.

Miss Coronation – Sheila Corcoran – joined in a Coronation procession around Aylesbury accompanied by her maids of honour.

Dogfight Days

IT was a battle no one wanted.

But when it was announced in 1969 that a third London airport might be sited at Wing – which would have certainly meant the complete destruction of the village of Cublington near Aylesbury – local people, backed by MPs and stars of television, radio and the cinema, rose up in anger.

'They marched to the strains of Land of Hope and Glory', it was reported of a demonstration which took place in Aylesbury on a sweltering hot day in July of that year when 1,500 marched through the town

The march had been timed to take place 24 hours before the start of the Roskill Commission inquiry in to the use of the site, which was being held in the town.

In the coming weeks the local newspapers were to devote many column inches to extensive reporting of the inquiry.

And all along the way the protests continued.

On that July day in the centre of Aylesbury there was a succession of speakers 'who included composer and arranger John Dankworth and his wife, jazz singer Cleo Laine, who recently moved into Bucks; the author Geoffrey Household, who lives near the proposed site of the airport and Lady Barlow, actress Margaret Rawlings.

'Actress Patricia Neal, and her husband Roald Dahl, who live at Great Missenden, also joined the speakers on the platform towards the end of the proceedings,' it was reported.

Mr Dankworth told those attending: "It is preposterous and stupid that a way of life should be so disturbed to satisfy the needs of a few years of aviation history."

And a letter of support was received which read: "This is a monstrous development that would destroy the quality of life and the amenities of the area which have been enjoyed for countless years."

It had been written by Robert Maxwell who, at the time, was MP for Buckingham.

A number of groups had been set up to fight the proposal, the largest being WARA (the Wing Airport Resistance Association) and this received whole-hearted support from the Poet Laureate, Sir John Betjeman.

Giving evidence to the inquiry, held at the Borough Assembly Hall, Sir John said 'only Stansted would be a worse choice than Wing for an aerodrome near to London which would destroy the peace of a maximum amount of genuine English landscape'.

More than 80 societies, both local and national, along with nearly 100 parish councils opposed the plans which were eventually shelved.

'Combines not Corcorde' was the message at this protest march against the third London airport being sited at Wing.

Local clergy, on behalf of their parishioners, joined the airport protests and crowds cheered as this 'effigy' of the Roskill Commission report went up in flames.

Singer Cleo Laine took to the stage – backed by her husband John Dankworth and his band – to lend her voice to the protests.

Wherever they were held there was always massive support for protest meetings organised by WARA – the Wing Airport Resistance Association.

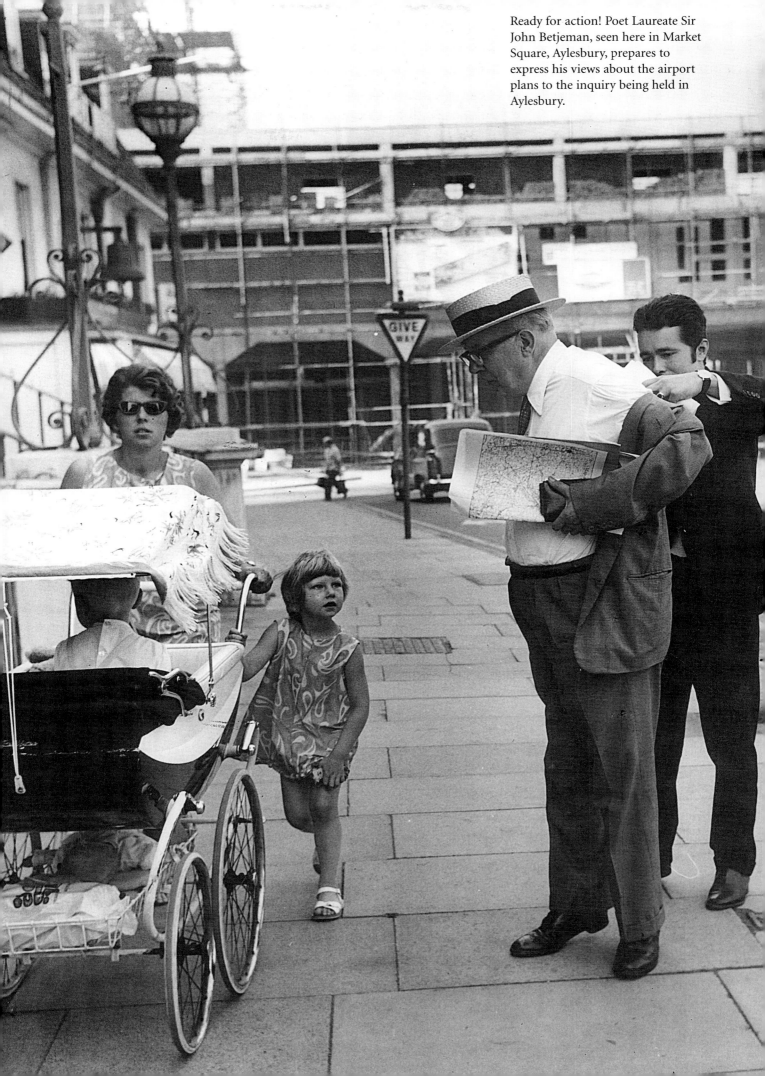

Ready for action! Poet Laureate Sir John Betjeman, seen here in Market Square, Aylesbury, prepares to express his views about the airport plans to the inquiry being held in Aylesbury.

Villainy in the Vale

'DARING BANDITS HOLD UP NIGHT MAIL FLYER'. This was the front page headline in *The Bucks Herald* of Friday, 9 August 1963 which appeared the day after what was described as 'a brilliantly planned ambush' by 'commando-style bandits' who had pulled off the biggest and most daring train robbery in history.

It was to become known as 'The Great Train Robbery' or 'The Crime of the Century' and, through Press coverage, took the name of Aylesbury – where the robbers were tried and sentenced – around the world.

To begin with it was thought the haul from the Royal Mail train travelling from Scotland to Euston, amounted to a million pounds.

It was later to be revealed that the early morning raid had netted the gang around £2.5 million in old bank notes.

The train was ambushed at Sears Crossing, Cheddington.

'Methods used by the raiders indicated that some of them had railway know-how', it was reported.

'So thoroughly was the ambush planned that the robbers had even taken the trouble to mark the track with white cloths at the point where they expected the train to stop,' the report continued.

For a time it looked as though they might have got away with it but, because the money was 'too hot to handle' they had decided to hide-out not far from the scene of the crime at Leatherslade Farm, Brill, the Bucks Police Force, as it was known at the time, having been tipped off that something suspicious was going on there by a local herdsman.

More than 40 policemen surrounded the farm but there was no one there.

Officers clambered through an upstairs window and made their way to the cellar where they found sacks stuffed with money from all the major High Street banks.

But it was only part of their massive haul, the remainder had disappeared.

Aylesbury soon became the centre of the nation's biggest-ever manhunt and while the farm itself was carefully checked for fingerprints, just as the rail coaches themselves had been, police were also carrying out an equally detailed investigation with local boys.

They were checking with them to see if any had noted down the car numbers of any vehicles seen in the area of the farm.

'Many of the children in the area collect car numbers and the police are interviewing every one of them who might have been jotting down numbers during the past week,' *The Bucks Herald* reported.

Rumours were rife among 'locals' that the Leatheslade Farm itself had a murky past having been the hide-out of a German spy during the war!

Two weeks after the raid the arrests began and it was revealed that at the farm police had found 'enough provisions to feed a small army' including 170 eggs, 33 tins of baked beans, 19 tins of pork luncheon meat, knives and forks for up to 16 people and even 34 toilet rolls!

Arrests continued and the trial began on 20 January 1964.

The committal took place in the Aylesbury Rural District Council Chamber in Walton Street, because the Bucks Assizes building in the centre of the town was not large enough to accommodate the 20 accused along with 30 barristers and five rows of Press seats. The story was reported around the world.

A special dock had to be built for the 20 accused who included Charles Wilson, James Hussey, Douglas Goody, Robert Welch, Roy James, also known as The Weasel and, of course Ronnie Biggs. (Biggs escaped after serving only 15 months of his 30 year sentence, went to live in Rio de Janeiro and was only to return 35 years later – something which brought memories flooding back for many Aylesbury people).

It was estimated each robber had at least a £100,000 share from the robbery. The court saw more than 600 exhibits and heard a total of 240 witnesses over a five week period.

It brought considerable business to the town with lawyers, police and the Press taking all the accommodation available in local hotels and with those who provided bed-and-breakfast.

In one local pub – known then as the Old Millwrights Arms in Walton Street, Aylesbury – a large wooden plaque was put up, with a train carved across the top, and many of those who ate and drank there during the investigation and the trial signed their names below it.

After a 58-day trial, sentence was passed at the Bucks Assizes held in Market Square and those responsible for writing the name of Aylesbury into the records of historic crime received a total of 573 years imprisonment.

Five years later Aylesbury became the centre of attention again when fugitive robber Bruce Reynolds, who was believed to be one of the ring leaders but who had spent some years abroad, was sentenced to 25 years in prison for his part in the heist.

When charged, Reynolds replied: 'C'est la vie' – 'That's life'.

Wherever they were taken – whether to committal proceedings which took place at Linslade, or at their trial in Aylesbury – those charged with The Great Train Robbery tried to hide from the public and there was always a heavy police guard.

On the scene. Police photographer John Bailey captures 'on camera' the mail train coaches which were raided at Sears Crossing.

A simple device and a glove found at the scene which were used to change the signalling and stop the Royal Mail train.

Standing at Cheddington station, where they were taken following the robbery, some of the coaches which housed the millions of pounds in cash.

The scene outside the Rural District Council offices in Aylesbury as the defendants arrived for trial.

Waiting outside the Bucks Assizes in Market Square, Aylesbury, to hear what sentences had been passed on The Great Train Robbers.

The Press were kept constantly up-to-date on how the police were getting on in their investigations into 'The Crime of the Century' outside Leatherslade Farm.

No stone was left unturned to find those who had carried out the Great Train Robbery, even areas of the garden at Leatherslade Farm were examined.

Rumours were rife about what had been going on at Leatherslade Farm… and 'locals' wanted to know more.

How 'The Crime of the Century' was reported in the *Bucks Herald*.

Sporting Talent

Skipper of Haddenham United, Freddie Hopkins, is hoisted high by enthusiastic team mates after the team's victory in the Good Friday Field Shield competition, played on the Aylesbury United ground, in 1952. They beat Wingrave, 4-2.

Bierton's triumphant team after winning the Oving Village Cup in 1953.

Over 6,000 spectators turned up to see the biggest match ever to be staged at Aylesbury's stadium and the most talked about for 20 years – Aylesbury v Wycombe in the FA Cup. Attendance beat the ground record by over 3,000. The game ended in a draw – 2-2 – so all those who had come along had to wait for the replay.

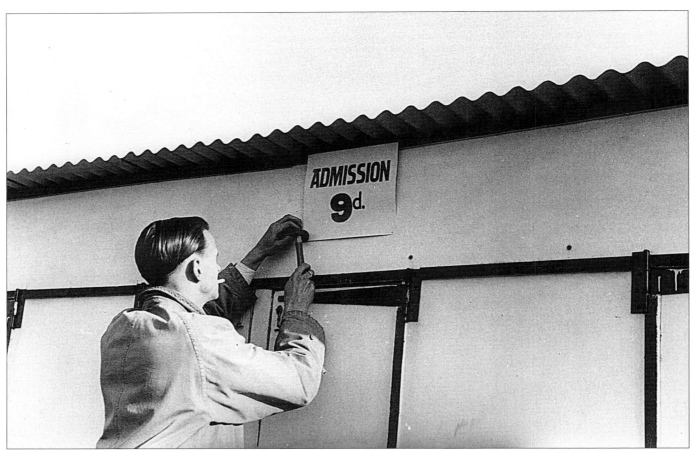

A lot of preparation went in to preparing the Aylesbury United ground in October 1950 for their FA Cup match against Wycombe – rolling the ground and, is that an increase in the admission charge we see (top picture)?

Aylesbury United were bottom of the Delphian league when they took on the mighty Hendon, top Athenian club, in front of a crowd of 4,500 in November 1951. It was a thrill-a-minute match resulting in a 4-3 win for Aylesbury, knocking Hendon out of the FA Cup. Eric Wells and Jock McCullum scored two each for Aylesbury and the town's Mayor, Mrs K.M. White met the team.

It was a hard fought match but in May 1953, Aylesbury United were able to add the Berks and Bucks Benevolent Cup to their previous success as runners-up in the Delphian League.

Set for the Senior Cup semi-final at Wolverton, fans filled extra carriages on the train but there was little to blow trumpets about on the way home as Aylesbury lost 3-2 to Chesham United in their match which took place in March 1948.

Look out for No. 54 – Billy Austin of Tring, the eventual winner – seen here at the 'push off' for the 350cc race at the motor cycle races on the old airfield site at Long Marston in April 1953.

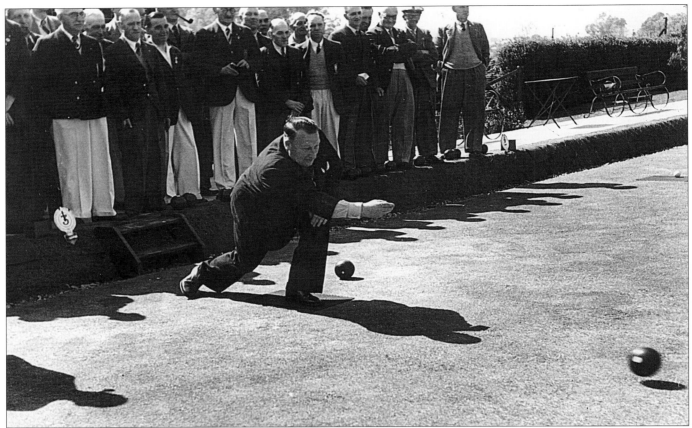

Opening the Hazells Bowling Green in Aylesbury in May 1948 – for the use of staff from Hazell Watson and Viney, printers and bookbinders – the Mayor, Cllr C.G. Cousins just could not resist having a go.

Here's how you do it properly! A training night in October 1953 for juniors of the Aylesbury and District Boxing Club.

Tony Picot, aged 14 and weighing 6st 8lbs, a pupil of The Grange School, Aylesbury, is pictured in April 1957 being cheered by fellow pupils after winning the title of Junior School Boy Boxing Champion of Great Britain at the Empress Hall, London.

It was a day especially for workers at printers Hazell Watson and Viney in Aylesbury, their families and friends – Hazells Sports Day. As the picture shows there was always a large turnout to watch events including a boxing display organised by the Aylesbury and District Boxing Club.

Further action from the Hazell Watson and Viney Sports Day: cycling when, at this event held in 1954, Aylesbury Cycle Club beat Finsbury Park and athletics, below.

From Rats to Riches

Described by Mrs Beeton in the first edition of *The Book of Household Management,* published in 1861, as 'deservedly a universal favourite' the Aylesbury duck was known around the world.

And much of this was owed to members of the Weston family.

Pictured above is William James Weston – known simply as 'Ducky' Weston – being interviewed for Canadian radio in 1954, just one of the countries where the family name was well known, others including Australia, America and even China.

He had begun taking an active part in the trade while still a schoolboy by helping his father at their duck farm in Mount Street, Aylesbury.

He went on to take over the 'Duckery' when his father died and immediately inherited the nickname 'Ducky' by which not only his father but also his grandfather and great-grandfather had been known.

It is on record that 'Ducky' and his father could kill and pluck six ducks in just 10 minutes!

He died six years after this broadcast was made, two weeks after his 70th birthday, and his only son, also named William Weston took over the business and is pictured (left) acting as a judge at a locally held competition.

He was the last in the family to be involved in the breeding of Aylesbury ducks, so ending a 200-year-old tradition.

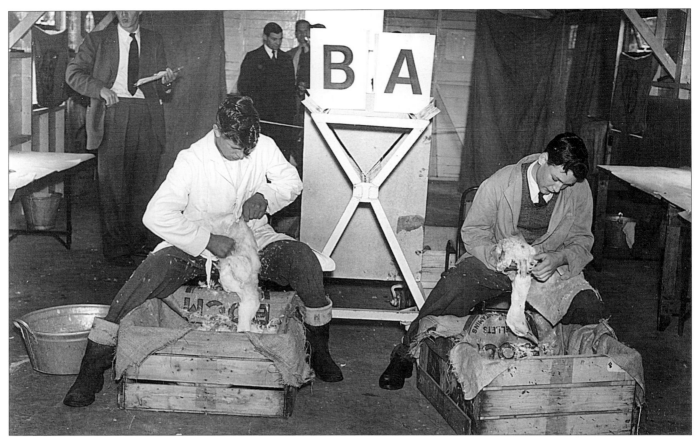

This picture shows two local competitors (Freddie Sanford, left and John Restall, right) taking part in the National Duck Plucking Championships held in July 1954 at the British Oil & Cake Mills (BOCM) site in Risborough Road, Stoke Mandeville.

Children enjoying the open air swimming pool at The Vale Park, Aylesbury, during the Whitsun holiday in May 1959.

The proudest man in Speen in 1947 was the sub postmaster, Mr George Ridgley who, at the age of 92, was awarded an MBE for long and faithful service.

The award was the culmination of 44 years service as village postmaster and over 25 years in the additional role of postman, not only for Speen but also the surrounding villages.

Mr Ridgley also held the distinction of being the oldest sub postmaster in the country.

'For 25 years, whatever the weather, he never failed to carry out his one delivery a day, a task that involved a 10-mile walk over a scattered and hilly district. To a non-smoker, who never had a cigarette or pipe, this did not prove a problem,' it was reported.

A long wait is in store for the youngsters pictured here during a scorching hot day in June 1947 to get in to The Vale open air swimming pool in Aylesbury... but, as one of the only cool spots in the town, it had to be worth it.

Rats were a problem in areas of Aylesbury in 1946 but the town had its own 'hit squad' – Mr Sid Skoyles and members of his 'Underground Movement' seen here 'baiting a sewer during the Southcourt Rat War'. Twenty-five rats 'of all shapes and sizes' lie in front of their former sewer home.

The local smithy, once a familiar sight but now rarely seen, is remembered here with this photograph, taken in March 1954, of Stanley Kirk at his Oving forge.

In June 1950 more than 750 pensioners called in to Aylesbury Town Hall to collect food parcels which had been given by the Australian government – the largest distribution of parcels in one day, above. Although rationing had ended after the war, life was still a struggle for many and the gift parcels, which included tins of food and bars of soap, were very welcome.

The following year parcels were still being distributed – in Aylesbury alone more than 30,000 were received – as shown in our picture, below, taken at Queen's Park School where 300 were given to pupils by the headmaster, Mr P Jones.

It was October 1957 and there was controversy after plans were announced for a road widening scheme in Walton Road, Aylesbury which would have meant this butchers shop, owned by Mr George Osterfield, being 'chopped in two', the front disappearing but the rear of the shop being left standing. The Ministry of Transport ruled that the shop could be compulsorily purchased by Aylesbury Borough Council.

A familiar sight around Aylesbury and the surrounding district – and a very welcome one during the 'Indian Summer' of 1948 as our picture taken at Bierton shows – was Plested's Ices arriving by motor bike and sidecar.

Caught on the other side of the camera was Alex Weston, chief photographer of *The Bucks Advertiser* for many years, when the BBC visited Aylesbury to broadcast a programme about life in the town – and who better to speak to but the man who had recorded so much of it on film?

A shooting party out for the day at Wooton Lake near Aylesbury in January 1946. And with a 'bag' of 300 rabbits throughout the day, the skinned animals could be sold for 3d each, the pelts for 1d apiece.

A well known smiling and soot smeared face around the Aylesbury district was Harry Pipe – 'chimney sweep by trade' – who was caught on camera during his rounds in September 1958. Having been a chimney sweep since he was a lad he continued in his trade when he came to Aylesbury from London during World War Two.

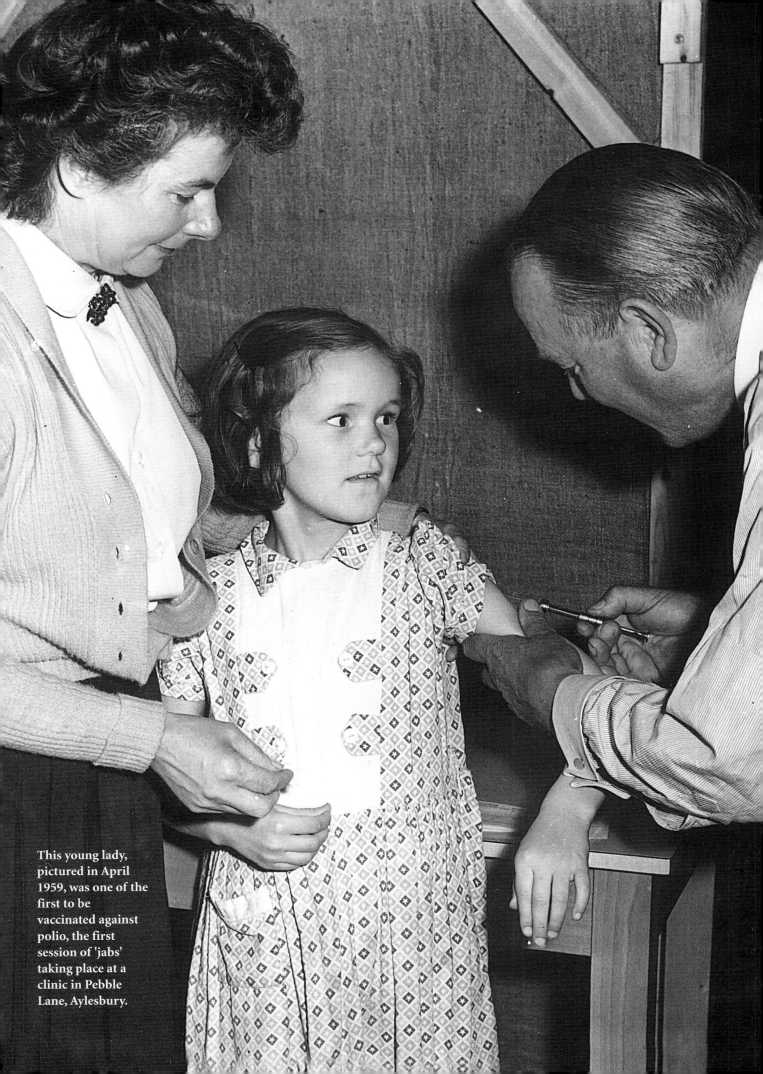

This young lady, pictured in April 1959, was one of the first to be vaccinated against polio, the first session of 'jabs' taking place at a clinic in Pebble Lane, Aylesbury.

The roar of traffic along busy Walton Street in Aylesbury was silenced for several minutes one afternoon in July 1956 when a swan – thought to have come from either the Oxford Road brook or the canal – was found running loose. The strong arm of the law was brought in and the distraught bird was 'arrested' and handed over to the RSPCA. On the left of the picture is the former Cogger & Hawkins garage.

In November 1956, Mrs Kirkham, wife of the village policeman, was known as Aston Clinton's traffic warden. Here she is seen watching over the safety of local children as they cross the busy trunk road on their way to and from school.

Signing on the dotted line for an 'adventure of a lifetime' – volunteers signing-up for a new Territorial Army unit in Aylesbury in January 1958.

The end of an era. Harry Clarke and Dolly, the last drawn dray of the Aylesbury Brewery Company (ABC) which at one time had its own brewery in Walton Street, Aylesbury, now the site of office and housing development.

The first woman police sergeant in Aylesbury – Irene Jones – found herself facing the camera while on traffic duty in Market Square in January 1953 before the opening of the Bucks Assizes.

Perhaps it was a week short of news, or maybe just a shot of men at work that the photographer could not resist. Whatever the reason, it has placed on record the efforts of these men 'caught in action' clearing blocked drains in Buckingham Street, Aylesbury in 1959.

He was a familiar character, sitting on his favourite bench in Market Square, Aylesbury, smoking his pipe.

William Green – nicknamed 'Pigeon' Green after his father – is pictured here in 1950 when the local newspapers ran special articles to mark his 91st birthday which, it was thought, was on 22 July but it was discovered he was actually born two weeks earlier!

The reports read that he would often break in to song with the chorus of the old Buckinghamshire folk song *The Prickly Bush* and, when younger, would turn somersaults in the road for a copper. Also that, whatever the weather or season, he was never without a flower in his buttonhole.

Yet no one could recall where the nickname, 'Pigeon', came from. He died two years after this picture was taken.

Almost in the line of fire, the photographer 'shot' this picture on the firing range at Kimble used by members of the First Bucks Battalion of the Home Guard in March 1953, who were undergoing training in the use of Sten guns.

Long after World War Two ended many things were in short supply – including coal.

As our picture, above, taken in March 1947, shows, a priority for many people, young and old alike, was to turn up at a coal dump site in Aylesbury to collect, in whatever container they could find, their 'ration' of 28lbs of what was described in its day as 'black magic'. Six years later, in 1953, below, things had changed very little and local people were still turning up to collect their coal.

And so, after the war years, came the clearing up operation. A bomb disposal squad, above, was called in during June 1957 to clear Ivinghoe Beacon of shells left by troops who used the area as a practice range. When found they had to be disposed of safely and Sgt Jimmy Slack, below, leader of the squad is seen holding two mortar bombs and behind him is the pit in which a total of 19 'missiles' were exploded.

The sign tells its own story – 'No Coupons'. Pictured in May 1950, it was used to mark the day that petrol coupons were thrown away.

Happy days! An outing for children from Mount Street, Aylesbury, described simply in the '50s newspaper of the day as 'kids off to the hills'.

What a crack shot! Lord Lieutenant of Bucks, Lord Cottesloe was president of the Bucks County Rifle Association in 1952 and, at the age of 90 – having had a lifelong interest in rifles and who, when young, had been a member of a rifle team from Eton which won the public schools championship at Wimbledon – scored a bull from 20 yards to mark the opening of the association's new ranges at Wendover.

With the end of rationing no one minded queuing, even for sweets as this 1949 picture shows, taken outside the 'High Class Confectioner & Tobacconist', L.J. Ratter in High Street, Aylesbury.

What are they doing? Believe it or not this was all part of a traditional ceremony, called Beating the Bounds, which many parishes carried out each year to ensure that everyone knew 'the bounds', or boundary, of their own parish. This picture, taken in 1952, shows a group from Grendon Underwood who were taking part also in what was known as Rogationtide which was linked to a successful harvest. Here Bill George turned young Peter Perrin upside-down while Alan Young adds a playful pat with a spade. As part of the tradition those taking part also cut crosses in the turf and made marks on gates to signify they had been there.

It was certainly an outing to remember when a party of 660 from the Walton Parish in Aylesbury left the town by special train for a visit to a London circus in February 1959.

Not seen in Aylesbury for a long time, a queue was quick to form at this stall in the open air market in Market Square on a rainy day in May 1948. What were they so keen to buy, and taste? Pineapples!

With their own club premises in Britannia Street, Aylesbury, 170 staff from printers and bookbinders Hazell Watson and Viney Ltd, which was based in the town, are seen here attending a social and dinner in December 1956.

Aylesbury became the centre of carpet making for the first time in 1951 – when this picture was taken – when William Goodacre and Sons Ltd, manufacturers of carpets since 1863 and among the first to use automatic looms, established a factory at Park Mill in Bicester Road which had once been a hat factory. About 80 people worked there and production of carpets, mostly for the export market, was nearly 100 a week.

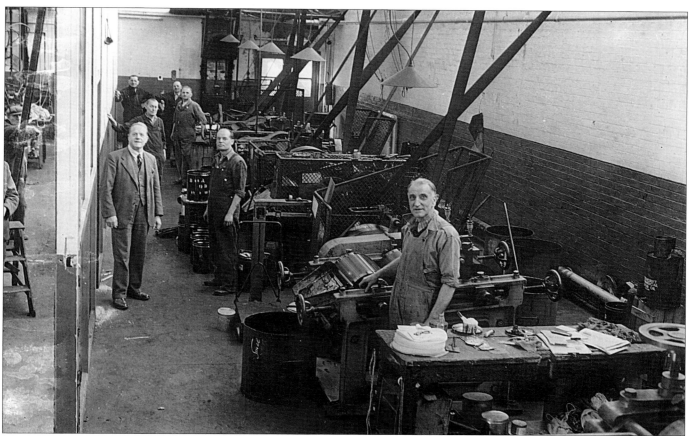

When this picture was taken in 1952, Aylesbury could boast its own ink works, which, to be found on the California estate close to the railway station in the town, was used to produce ink for printers and bookbinders Hazell Watson and Viney Ltd.

Millions of small but very essential accessories for planes and tanks – mainly using tiny pieces of metal and bakelite – were produced during World War Two at the Argo Electrical Company premises in Aylesbury. In this 1945 picture workers are seen carrying out the delicate work.

Leading manufacturer of agricultural machinery, New Holland, opened a new factory on the Gatehouse estate in Aylesbury in September 1961. Covering 62,000 square feet on a ten-acre site, over 48,000 square feet of factory, which no longer exists, was devoted solely to manufacture so that the company could provide a wider range of products.

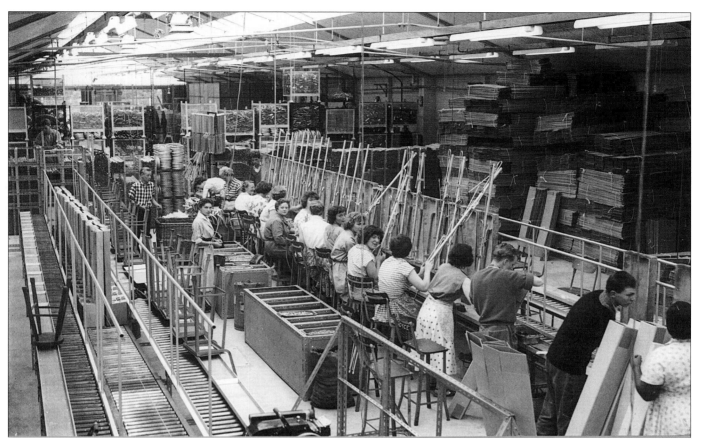

The largest manufacturer of television aerials in Europe, Antiference Ltd, opened a new factory in Bicester Road, Aylesbury in August 1957. The 400 workers, above, could produce an average of 8,000 aerials a day. The factory, which has since closed, was opened by MP for Aylesbury Sir Spencer Summers who was welcomed by staff who lined the route to the main entrance.

There was a 17-year-old look-a-like of film star Diana Dors – Gloria Haig – Donald Gray and Avis Scott who were appearing at the time on television and Miss Anona Winn, known for her appearances on the programme *Twenty Questions*. They all turned up to support the Trades Fair held at the Town Hall (pictured here) and Hazells Hall in Aylesbury town centre, which had been organised by the Aylesbury Chamber of Commerce in September 1954.

With fuel for home fires at a premium, there was a good trade to be had in woodcutting and, in 1946, this industrious person was caught on camera at Hardwick.

With the grand name of 'a centrifugal casting unit' – the only one of its kind in Europe – new machinery was installed at the Hazell Watson and Viney printing works in Aylesbury in May 1957, above, but only after a member of staff had taken what, in those days, was the unusual step of travelling to America to see how the unit worked and to make sure that it would be beneficial to the company. The unit cast lead in to moulds more efficiently and to those working at the factory in the composing room, below, that was vitally important.

Craftsmen at Air Trainers Ltd, in Bicester Road, Aylesbury, created this model, above, of Sir Francis Drake's famous galleon, The Golden Hind, to take part in the Coronation procession through the town in 1953.

One-sixth of the size of the original vessel the model was an exact replica, 17ft 6ins long, 15ft high and 4ft wide. It weighed half a ton.

It was 'launched' by the Mayoress of Aylesbury, Mrs A.J. Sage, below, in the customary fashion – a bottle of champagne being smashed across its bow. Later it was given to the town by its makers and was given a place of honour on a balcony in the Town Hall.

He may well have been one of the last of his kind. Pictured in May 1946 is Mr H.J. Taylor hard at work at the LMS Basket Works in Park Street, Aylesbury where, at that time, he was the only employee. Basket weaving was a trade well known in and around the town, most of it linked with the transport of the town's most famous commodity, the Aylesbury duck to the London markets. In the main the baskets were made of willow which was grown locally on what were known as osier beds.

The Nestle Milk Company in High Street, Aylesbury, produced its last bottle of milk at midday on Tuesday, 31 October 1961 and our photographers were there to record the event.

At one stage the output at the factory was around 10,000 gallons a day. The end of the 'pinta' production made way for the building of a five-storey block that joined the existing factory to cater for the rapid expansion of their soup business which continues today.

Dame Margot Fonteyn is obviously delighted to see her husband, Dr Roberto Arias leaving the National Spinal Injuries Centre at Stoke Mandeville in February 1966 , where the Panamanian diplomat had been since an attempt on his life in Panama.

Seeing him off is deputy matron Miss M .C. Dyke. The night before he left, Dr Arias organised a private party for staff members as a token of his thanks. During his time in hospital famous visitors included Senator Robert Kennedy and film star John Wayne who, said Dame Margot 'just came charging in to the hospital'.

Each year it was a case of 'all hands to the spoon' as nurses at St John's Hospital at Stone joined in to help with the mixing of Christmas puddings for more than 1,000 people – patients, staff and visitors to the hospital. In our 1956 picture it is the Matron, Miss C.H. Mitchell, offering some of her nurses a taste of the mixture.

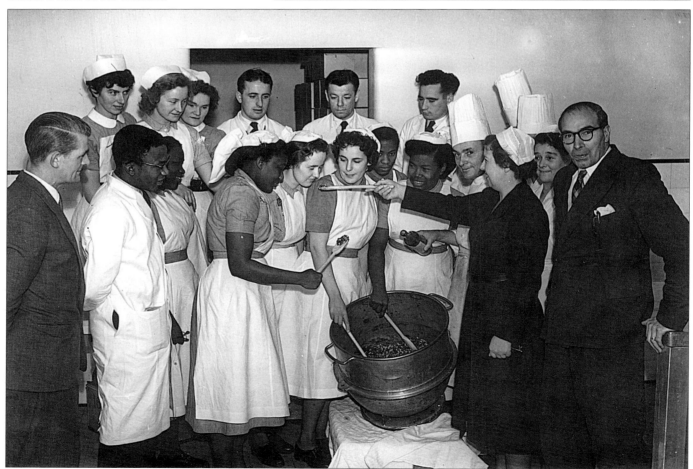

Basketball has always been one of the favourite sports at the National Stoke Mandeville Games as this picture, taken in 1958 – the early days of the games – goes to prove.

Film star Kenneth Moore was 'delighted' to accept an invitation to attend the seventh Stoke Mandeville Games in 1958 to award the prizes to the wheelchair athletes. He is pictured with Sir Ludwig Guttmann, founder of the games.

There were plenty of bouquets to be given out to senior staff of the Aylesbury District Group Hospital Nursing School after they had watched as their student nurses received awards at a prize giving ceremony held at Stoke Mandeville Hospital in 1953.

To help spinal patients at Stoke Mandeville Hospital a new bus – with ramps – was presented to the hospital by the British Legion and London Transport in 1948.

Surrounded by large areas of open land – unlike today – basketball competitors are pictured at the 1957 Stoke Mandeville Games.

Learning new skills, especially arts and crafts, has long been looked upon as good therapy as this picture, taken at Stoke Mandeville Hospital in June 1946, with patients learning a variety of occupational skills, clearly shows.

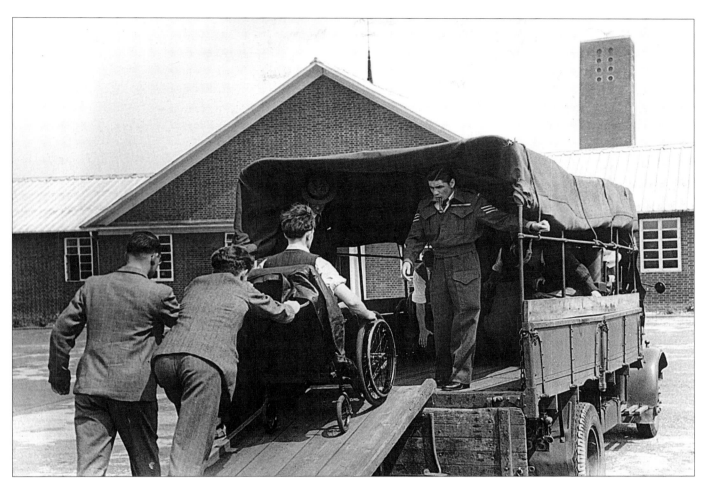

Previous page and above: Here we go chaps! Spinal patients at Stoke Mandeville Hospital were taken on a tour of the area in July 1947 on an outing arranged by the local branch of the Electrical Trades Union and members of the International Alloys Social Club in the town – Alloys, as it was known, being one of the largest employers in Aylesbury at the time.

No wonder they are smiling! These nurses, pictured in 1956, have just successfully completed their three years' training at Stoke Mandeville Hospital.

Mayhem, Mishaps and Disasters

It was headlined as being 'the worst fire Aylesbury has seen for 50 years' – the day in September 1963 that fire destroyed warehouses on the site of printers and bookbinders Hazell Watson and Viney in Victoria Street and threatened nearby homes. At one time flames were up to 50 feet high, homes had to be evacuated and the area was cordoned off. Fourteen hours later the charred remains of the warehouse were still smouldering.

More than 200 people turned up to watch after the 18th century Hartwell House, between Aylesbury and Stone, caught fire in July 1963. But they did not stand around watching for long. After a plea for help many of them joined in a bid to rescue furniture, paintings and valuables from the burning building which at the time was a finishing school for around 80 girls who, only hours before fire broke out, had left for their summer holidays.

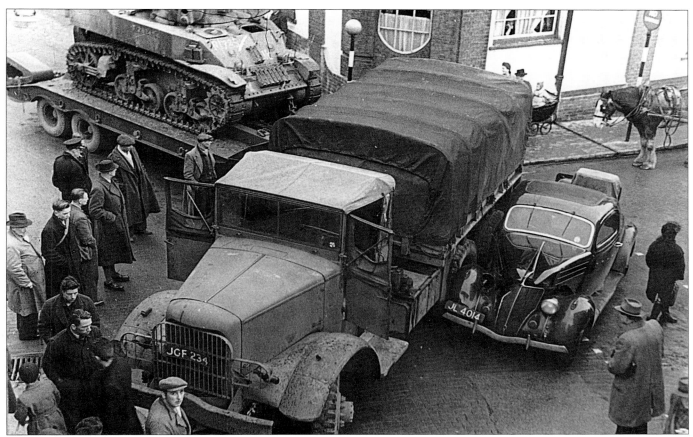

Walton Street in Aylesbury was impassable for over half-an-hour one day in January 1948 when a lorry, pulling a trailer and tank, was in collision with a car. Fortunately no one was injured.

It looked worse than it was! A steam engine of a goods train overshot the buffers on a siding between Wendover and Halton in February 1958, and plunged down a nearby embankment.

The driver was badly shaken but escaped unhurt and damage to the engine was only slight.

In December 1953 the biggest fire since the war gutted Aylesbury Grammar School and much of the building facing Walton Road was reduced to a shell. The cause of the fire was an electrical fault and items lost in the blaze, which mainly affected the area of the main hall, were the founders' portraits, war memorial tablets and trophies.

It is March 1952 and a bulldozer moves in to begin demolishing what is left of the Town Hall, Aylesbury, following a disastrous fire.

Surrounding buildings in London Road, Aston Clinton, suffered heat damage when a toy factory was destroyed by fire in June 1950.

Double-decker passengers to High Wycombe had a long delay following this accident at Kimble, close to the Bernard Arms, in 1952.

A lorry carrying earth was in collision with two stationary and unoccupied cars before overturning and spilling its load at the junction of Weedon Road with Cromwell Avenue in September 1961.

When the Red Rover bus pictured here skidded on an icy road at Oving one evening in February 1947, 16 passengers were hurt and one was detained in hospital. The bus was coming round a corner when it fell 'broadside' into a field.

Carrying seven tons of tiles, this lorry skidded on an icy road at Brewery Hill, Rowsham in January 1959 and crashed into a tree.

The drivers of these vehicles – which after the crash attracted a lot of interest from local children – were lucky to escape following a collision at the junction of Carrington Road and Lee Road, Southcourt, Aylesbury, in August 1958.

Fire broke out in a downstairs room of 37, Weston Road, Aston Clinton on a Monday afternoon in January 1946 and firemen, who had been alerted by the owner who escaped uninjured, found on their arrival they had to deal with an exploded gas meter.

Wreckage was scattered across three fields after a Canberra jet bomber crashed at Wiggington in March 1957. 'The plane passed low over the village in a mist and struck the ground, ploughing a flaming furrow across the soil and through the hedges', it was reported. The aircraft was a training flight and the three airmen on board were killed.

It was the new headquarters of the Aylesbury Darby and Joan club but it could not stand up to the terrific storm which hit the area in November 1957. High winds and heavy rain tore off chimney stacks, twisted TV aerials, ripped up trees and blew roofs off sheds and buildings, including the club.

The driver of this 24-ton milk tanker, which skidded and overturned at the Bugle Horn corner at Hartwell, near Aylesbury in February 1963, escaped unhurt. But the main road was blocked for some time until heavy breakdown equipment could be brought in to winch the tanker clear.

Not a lot was moving along this road at Whitchurch in March 1947 thanks to heavy snow falls.

Heavy rain and melting snow which had fallen over the previous few weeks resulted in heavy flooding in many parts of Aylesbury in March 1947.

Freak weather struck at Low Farm, Haddenham early one November morning in 1963 when a gale force wind ripped off the roof of the farmhouse – the roof then falling back down on the house causing considerable damage. At the time the occupants were downstairs and escaped unhurt. Not so fortunate were some of their chickens when one of the wooden chicken houses at the farm was demolished by the wind.

Screen and Screams

Film star Michael Wilding is pictured here in September 1948 attending the annual fête, of the Princes Risborough branch of the British Legion.

Motor racing champion Stirling Moss visited the town in October 1952 to present a trophy to Angela Wood, winner of a Miss Aylesbury competition.

It was gala day in Church Square, Long Crendon, on 23 May 1953 and there was a special guest to judge the Miss Crendon competition – actor Laurence Olivier.

Only too delighted to sign autographs were Laurence Olivier and his wife, Vivien Leigh, who lived locally, when they attended a fête, at Chilton organised by the Aylesbury West Agricultural Club in June 1947.

Known to radio listeners as 'Mrs Waters' famous daughters', Gert and Daisy would not let the rain dampen their spirits when they joined in the fun of the St Leonard's Church fête, held in the village of St Leonard's, in September 1947.

Oops, steady does it! Radio personality Dennis Noble was the guest at the 1947 Wilstone Show but discovered it was not as easy as he had first thought to ride a donkey which seemed to have a mind of its own.

Jackie Kennedy and her sister, Princess Lee Radziwell were caught on camera outside The Bell Inn, Aston Clinton, in May 1965 after lunching with Dr Roberto Arias, the Panamanian diplomat who had just come out of Stoke Mandeville Hospital.

He had spent 18 months there following an assassination attempt in his own country.

To the right, immediately behind Mrs Kennedy, is Michael Harris 'son of the proprietors who often saw Mrs Kennedy and the late president dining out in America, during his time training in that country'.

There was the chance for local people to ask *Twenty Questions* when the popular half-hour BBC radio programme, hosted by Richard Dimbleby, came live from the Town Hall, Aylesbury on 28 June 1957.

It was, we reported, 'a day of glorious chaos'.

A jet plane, which in fact had never left the ground, was made to appear as if it had crashed on 50 Buckingham Street, Aylesbury.

It was a life-size plywood model, left over from ATV's series *The Plane Makers* which was used in a location shoot for the TV drama series *Emergency-Ward 10* one chilly day in February 1966.

The plane had been brought to the town from the ATV studios at Elstree and was used in what turned out to be a 10 minute on-screen sequence broadcast the following day.

The scene was shot on the site of a former butchers slaughter house which was due for demolition.

It involved a total of 45 actors including 35 extras as well as more than 30 technical staff.

'The sequence was an ambitious one and called for spectacular special effects such as a wind machine, artificial smoke and some real flames,' it was reported.

One complete side of nearby Ripon Street was filled with a mobile control room and dressing rooms and three cameras were used.

Stars were Mark Eden, who played the pilot of the jet, Ian Cullen, Paul Barron and William Wilde who all scored a hit with the girls in the watching crowd, drawing whistles and screams as they went through their paces.

In February 1950 workers at Hazell Watson and Viney, printers and bookbinders, in Aylesbury, had 'a lunch time treat' – a visit from the BBC radio programme *Workers' Playtime*.

Above and previous page: It was a day many Aylesbury shoppers would never forget – Tuesday, 11 August 1953. The reason? They found themselves rubbing shoulders with actresses Glynis Johns and Diana Dors who were visiting the town for the day to film sequences in Market Square for *The Weak and the Wicked*. Their first scene was outside Weston's fashion shop and then the location moved to the lower part of the square, outside Barclays Bank.

Crowds were waiting in Market Square, Aylesbury, on this day in September 1948 to welcome actress Myrna Loy to the town when she arrived at County Hall, with a heavy police escort, to film scenes for *Autumn Violin*.

Much of MGM's epic *The Black Prince* was filmed at Tring Park, Tring in 1954 (shown in these four pictures) with Erroll Flynn in the title role and Peter Finch, his co-star, taking the part of a French knight.

Singer Petula Clark visited Aylesbury in October 1959 and took the opportunity to meet some of her local fans.

There is no mistaking this face, Jimmy Savile, of course, on a visit to the town in 1963, just one of so many he was to make as his work and support for Stoke Mandeville Hospital and the new National Spinal Injuries Centre there – which was built after he launched a £10 million appeal – has continued over the years.

She was certainly a hit with her young fans when singer Marion Ryan opened a new shop in the High Street, Aylesbury, in May 1958.

Nearly 3,000 teenagers turned up at the Granada in Aylesbury one night in February 1959 to see 'rock 'n' roll' star Cliff Richard on stage (above). After his performance more than 300 waited at the stage door hoping to meet him, one of the lucky ones being 15-year-old Jennifer Watkin from Halton (below).

On stage at The Granada in Aylesbury in January 1964 were the 'up and coming' group The Rolling Stones who were later interviewed for a broadcast to the apprentices at RAF Halton (below).

Lucky you! When Tommy Steele visited the Granada in Aylesbury in June 1961 he met one of his greatest fans, 15-year-old blind girl Wendy Sharpe who went to his dressing room, put her arm around him and gave him a big kiss… much to the envy of all his other fans waiting at the stage door who were not so lucky.

Eddie Friday at The Grosvenor and Borough Assembly Hall

Going wild at The Grosvenor in Aylesbury – a typical scene at the concerts held there where 'stars of the future' included Billy Fury, The Hollies and The Swinging Blue Jeans. But one couple seem oblivious to what is going on around them!

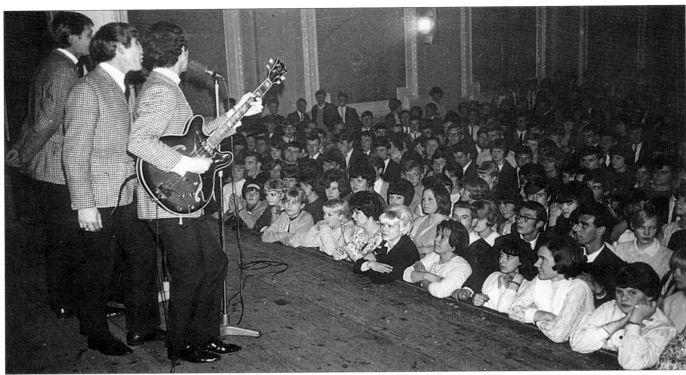

Among the successful groups to play in Aylesbury in their early days were The Barron Knights, the group members having strong local connections coming from Pitstone, Dunstable and Leighton Buzzard.

With their own brand of humour, which was their hallmark, they were an instant success in the town and are pictured on stage, above, and behind the scenes with concert promoter the late Eddie Friday who was to become a life-long friend of the group.

It was 'absolutely incredible' the impact that some of the singers and groups had on the audiences said Eddie Friday following a 1960s visit to the town of singer Englebert Humperdink, formerly the star Gerry Dorsey.

'I have special reason for remembering that night,' said Eddie in a later interview. 'The fans went wild and a number of them stormed on to the stage. Englebert was knocked to the ground and so was I when I tried to get order restored,' he said.

Later he threw pieces of the singer's shirt – which had already been torn – to anxious fans waiting in the Market Square.

But there is a story that pieces of the shirt went missing, only to turn up the next day being 'sold off' in the playground of a local school by an enterprising young man who managed to get to the shirt before Eddie did!

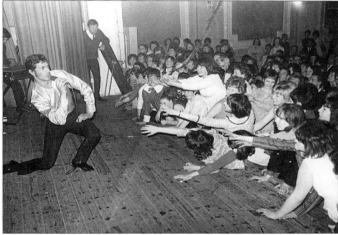

Making Hay

The Whaddon Chase Hunt at Oving in 1953.

Here the Old Berkeley Beagles are setting off from outside The Chandos at Weston Turville in December 1945.

The Old Berkeley West hunts some of the finest country in England, read the report of 19 January 1951, and this picture shows the chase in Hartwell Park with the Master of the foxhounds, Mrs H. Morton, leading the followers past the old mansion and heading across the Vale.

Moving off from outside The Red Lion and down the High Street at Wendover, this was the Old Berkeley West Hunt in January 1951.

Despite the rain these youngsters were determined to have fun at the Weston Turville gymkhana held in August 1956.

Donkey rides – organised by Charlie and Sheila Moorcroft – were a firm favourite at Wingrave fête, held in June 1956.

A loving pat on the neck for 'Silver' from three-year-old Elaine Workman of Long Marston, who took part in a leading rein class at the village gymkhana in May 1958.

Pony and trap rides were just one of the many attractions at a British Legion fête, held at Princes Risborough in 1953 to raise money for a new headquarters.

Good husbandry means everything to these members of the Aylesbury Borough Allotment and Garden Protection Society taking part in a Merrie England fair held in the town in April 1953.

There were some anxious faces amongst those competing for the grand challenge cup in a rabbit show organised as part of the Aylesbury Victory Garden Show and held in 1946.

It was certainly no yoke for these judges who needed to confer before making their decisions at the Bucks Rabbit and Poultry Society's Egg Show held in 1953.

This was a job where everyone mucked in – potato sowing at Wendover Farm in April 1948.

Colorado Beetle in Mid-Bucks in 1948 and Land Army girls were called in to help local farmers search out the pests and so combat the threat to potato crops. The worst outbreak recorded locally was at Quainton.

After months of rain the ground has dried, allowing this farmer at Stone, pictured in April 1951, to guide his team of horses as the harrow drags the ground.

A young farmer, just 16 years old, is pictured taking part in a Young Farmers Club ploughing match held at Long Crendon in 1953.

These two were caught on camera in 1953 while harvesting at Strawberry Hill off the Wendover to Great Missenden road.

Aylesbury became a 'foot and mouth controlled area' as a result of an outbreak of the disease in the area in 1954. Regular cattle markets were cancelled and only cattle under licence for slaughter were allowed to be moved.

Hay making at Rowsham during the summer of 1946.

There was always plenty of work for Land Army girls to do on farms in and around the Aylesbury area.

In all there were some 2,000 animals at the annual summer sheep fair held at Aylesbury cattle market off Exchange Street – now the site of a multi-screen cinema – in 1954. And, judging by the woman seated on top of one of the pens, it was quite a fashionable event as well!

October 1947, saw the sale of a herd of Ayrshire cattle by Mr J.A. de Rothschild at Home Farm, Waddesdon.

Keen interest was shown in mares and geldings at a sale organised on the site of Aylesbury cattle market in May 1946.

For many years Hartwell House at Stone hosted the Bucks County Show. This aerial picture, taken in 1953, not only shows events taking place at the show but, to the top left, the site of what, during the war years, had been a camp for Italian prisoners of war.

A little love and attention! Little Susan Bradnock carefully cleans her horses' hoof at the 1953 Bucks County Show.

Millionaire Mr N.S. Gulbenkian, president of the association responsible for organising the Bucks County Show, and show chairman Capt. J. Burrow-Hill, pictured walking around the showground in 1957.

This picture was taken from the roof of Hartwell House, Stone, showing the grand parade at the 1948 Bucks County Show.

Up and over! An action shot taken at the Bucks County Show in 1947.

Number 348 is 'Bucks Lass', led by Mr H. Brazier, which won the class for non pedigree cow, along with second prize in the open class, at the Bucks County Show held in 1947.

A Quieter Life

A picture which sums up a 'quieter life'. Villagers Will Frost and Arthur (nicknamed Autumn) Rose chatting on a spring day in 1949 by the village pump at Cuddington.

Taken in July 1956 this peaceful corner of Cuddington lies in the shadow of the parish church. The lone walker is farmer Alfred Millers of Holymans Farm.

With fresh produce – but not that much of it – brought down from London, people were only too happy to queue on the cobbles of Aylesbury market – the date, 8 December 1945, just weeks after the end of World War Two.

Work is going on here in February 1951 – in what was to become Churchill Avenue, Aylesbury – to create new council homes on the Southcourt estate.

In August 1959 work was well under way to create a by-pass for Great Missenden at a cost of £250,000.

One man and his dog (above) seen walking through the fields of Bedgrove Farm, on the outskirts of Aylesbury town, in May 1958. A year later (next two pictures) everything at the farm came under the auctioneer's hammer as the land and livestock were sold, the farmland later to become the Bedgrove housing estate which, when first completed, was the largest estate of private homes in the country.

Known as the Gate House, close to the centre of the town, above, and pictured in 1948, these buildings were to disappear to make way for what was to become the Gatehouse Estate in Aylesbury, work demolishing and clearing the Gate House itself being clearly shown in our 1955 picture, below.

Condemned by many 'towns folk' at the time they were built as a blot on the landscape, 'prefabs' at Quarrendon, Aylesbury had developed a charm of their own 'with trees and flowers blooming in front gardens which were formerly grazing ground for cattle', it was reported.

It was in 1955 that porter-signalman Alfred Saunderson got to work on the platform garden at Stoke Mandeville railway station in a bid to brighten it up.

That year he won third prize in the London Transport station garden competition. The following year, when this picture was taken, he took first prize and two years later he was awarded the challenge cup for the best garden in the whole of the London Transport region. And it is a success that the tiny Stoke Mandeville station has carried on ever since with others following in Mr Saunderson's footsteps.

These atmospheric shots of the centre of Aylesbury were taken on a misty morning in January 1953, above – a lone woman walking along Silver Street past The Dark Lantern public house which was owned by the Aylesbury Brewery Company. And she may have been making her way in to the nearby Market Square, below, where the statue of the Civil War hero John Hampden points towards his home at Great Hampden.

One little piggy went to the wrong market place in Aylesbury on Wednesday, 24 June 1953 after it managed to escape from the cattle market and ended up in Market Square where it disrupted traffic and run amok among the open air market stalls. After 30 minutes of freedom it was cornered in the yard of The Kings Head and locked in a barn until the owners could collect it. In the background is the shop of Jones & Cocks.

This is an unusual shot across the top of the Market Square, Aylesbury taken from Market Street, possibly around the time of a royal visit to the town. It is looking towards The Round House which still stands on the corner of both Cambridge Street and the High Street.

When the circus came to town in
October 1954, this elephant might have
thought the statue of the recumbent lion
– one of two in the Market Square,
Aylesbury (one asleep, the other awake) –
needed waking up. Or was it just a good
publicity stunt?

A busy scene in Market Square, Aylesbury in April 1953 – note the horse drawn cart ambling along beside the cars and motorbikes.

This charming scene, with the sunlight filtering through the trees, is of Dobbins Lane, Wendover and the land on either side has since been developed – but the avenue of trees is still there more than 50 years after this picture was taken in 1949.

A typical scene in Aylesbury on market day, pictured in 1959.

Local Press photographers find it hard not to take pictures of things simply because they are there, such as this row of cottages in Long Crendon which caught the cameraman's eye just after the war years.

A tiny corner of Dinton village taken in September 1947.

Every village has its stories to tell and Quainton, pictured here in 1948, is no different. For example, almshouses were built there for the 'poor widows and widowers of the parish' by the son of the principal secretary of state to King James 1, Richard Winwood. And that one of the former rectors of the church was Richard Brett, one of the 47 translators of the Bible in 1611. You would have known if you had read the local newspaper the week this picture appeared!

A quiet September scene taken in 1949 in the village of Haddenham.

Out for a late summer stroll, these two young ladies captured the eye of the cameraman in North Marston in 1957.

Half timbered houses, whitewashed walls and golden thatch – and a poster on the wall advertising what was being shown at The Granada cinema in Aylesbury, including *Fair Wind to Java* and *City That Never Sleeps*. The picture was taken in Weston Turville in 1953.

The peace and tranquility of the canal at Halton as it was in 1956.

This panoramic view was taken at Aston Clinton in 1952.

Owned, as so many pubs in the area were at one time by the Aylesbury Brewery Company, this was the Rose and Crown at Butlers Cross as it was in 1947. Sadly – again, like so many other pubs – it has disappeared.

The work of local blacksmith Mr Gilbert Grace, this picture, taken in 1947, shows an unusual gate at the entrance to a house at New Mill Tring which was almost opposite the flour mill, and which was skillfully worked in to the shape of numerous tools used in farming.

At one time one of the only links between Tring Road and Broughton Avenue in Aylesbury was this path – which was at the side of Adams garage – and was known simply as Coffee Lane. The picture was taken in 1958.

Waiting may be prohibited, as the sign says, but obviously not for this horse and trap spotted outside the Greyhound pub in Aylesbury one day in September 1947. One wonders where the horse's owner is?

Taken in 1963, this is a view of the historic Kings Head in Aylesbury town centre, which is owned by the National Trust, which most people will never have seen. Most of the frontage today is obscured by other buildings and the only part visible from the Market Square is the main entrance, approached along a narrow cobbled alleyway. It obviously proved too good an opportunity for one artist who chose to ignore the snow and the cold.

High above the roof tops of Aylesbury, Mr W. Wrighton – and an equally brave photographer – scaled the heights of St Mary's Parish Church in Aylesbury to 'put back the hands of time' in 1951.

Simple pleasures! This was how a small group of local youngsters entertained themselves in Walton Pond, Aylesbury in August 1949.

Unusual for its day, this aerial picture of Aylesbury, looking towards the town centre with the railway line running from left to right across the middle, and with part of the Southcourt Estate in the foreground, was taken in 1949.

A newcomer to Aylesbury would be unlikely to ever guess the location of these properties in the town. The taller of the three buildings was – and it is just possible to see the pub sign – the Hen and Chickens public house along the Oxford Road. The picture was taken in 1948. With road improvements having taken place it is still referred to by many 'locals' as the Hen and Chickens roundabout.

Pictured in 1947 is the Cambridge Street junction with New Street, Aylesbury. The pub on the corner was The Oddfellows Arms.

A 1947 view along Bourbon Street, Aylesbury clearly showing the public baths and, on the right, The Victoria public house. Much of the area on the left has become an entrance to the Friars Square shopping centre.

Parking restrictions in Aylesbury town centre are nothing new. This picture, taken in 1948, looks along Britannia Street, off the High Street. Just along the road, on the left, was the social club for the town's largest employer, printers and bookbinders Hazell Watson and Viney which was next to Marks & Spencer.

Pub names such as The Cross Keys and the Coach & Horses are clearly shown in this picture, taken from high on County Hall in Market Square, Aylesbury in 1950 looking in the direction of what is now the Friars Square shopping centre. Just behind the first row of houses was Silver Street and the picture was taken around the time when the town could boast of having up to 90 pubs!

Braving the icy conditions the photographer went to the top of the St Mary's Parish Church tower one day in February 1955 to capture this picture which shows Church Street on the left and looks out over the roof tops towards the Chiltern Hills.

A small area of Aylesbury town centre looking over Cambridge Street and the Upper Hundreds, taken in June 1955.

A custom which still survives – Morris Dancing – seen here outside the Crown & Thistle pub in Whitchurch in 1950.

Trains and Boats and Planes

On 31 January 1953 at 5pm the *Cheddington Flyer* made its last historic seven-mile journey from Aylesbury to Cheddington because 'after careful consideration' British Railways London Midlands Region felt that the passenger service, which first started in 1839, should be withdrawn. Hundreds of people queued for tickets wanting to be a passenger on the last train.

A MET 'tanker' engine had not stood in Quainton station for over 50 years and 250 railway enthusiasts made the trip in May 1954 behind the 62-year-old engine from Moorgate Station just for old time's sake.

The rail line between Aylesbury and Cheddington was blocked for over three hours on 11 October 1957 after this train was derailed at Stocklake during a shunting operation.

Over 6,000 people travelled from around the country in September 1969 for a steam weekend organised at the Quainton Road station.

Taken early in the 1950s this is a view of the Aylesbury arm of the Grand Union Canal looking towards the canal basin which is in the centre of the town.

For many years the canal in Aylesbury was a hive of industrious activity as this picture, taken in 1952 and showing the narrowboat *Roger* owned by A. Harvey-Taylor, clearly shows.

100 boats – and their owners of course – made the journey to Aylesbury in August 1961 for an annual boat rally staged by the Inland Water Association. Boats filled the canal basin in Aylesbury and stretched for a quarter of a mile along both sides of the canal. At the official close of the rally, the biggest ever at the time, 160 people sat down to an Aylesbury duck dinner.

Mayor of Aylesbury, Cllr Mrs Zena Williams, launched the new 'vessel' of the Aylesbury Sea Cadet Corps' at Canal Wharf, Walton Street, Aylesbury in March 1959 with a bottle of lemonade and then went for a trip along the canal in the boat named *Trusty*.

More than 100 children from Quainton went on an outing to the pantomime in 1948 with Keith Coaches.

Traffic jams are nothing new. This was the scene in Walton Street, Aylesbury, one day in July 1958 as vehicles made their way to the Silverstone race track.

Providing the commentary for a BBC television programme in 1952 on hill climbing at Aston Hill near Wendover – which gave its name to the Aston Martin which had its trial runs there – was TV personality Raymond Baxter, far right.

Television cameras were perched on the hillside at Aston Hill near Wendover for the programme about hill climbing made in November 1952.

Those who were at Haddenham airfield – now an industrial estate – when the aerial picture, on the next page, was taken in 1949 had special reason to remember the war years. The airfield was, for four years, home to a special glider training school set up at what at the time was known as RAF Thame, on the orders of Winston Churchill. Among many other missions the glider pilots took part in the D-Day operations. But after the war there was a lighter use for much of the airfield site – for motor-cycle racing.

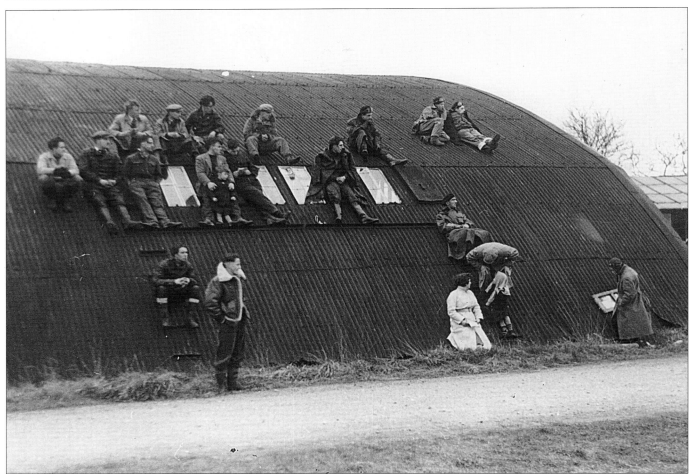

Previous page, top: On display at the government rocket propulsion research station at Westcott in 1947 were examples of the Germans V1 and V2 bombs and (bottom) Mr W.R. Cook, chief superintendent at Westcott was on hand to explain the intricate mechanisms of the giant bombs. Above: Shoppers in Aylesbury town centre were in for a surprise one day in September 1947 as a V2 bomb was slowly driven through the town. It was on its way to RAF Halton, for their Battle of Britain celebrations.

Aircraft on the ground were as big an attraction as those in the air for these youngsters attending the RAF Halton open day in September 1956.

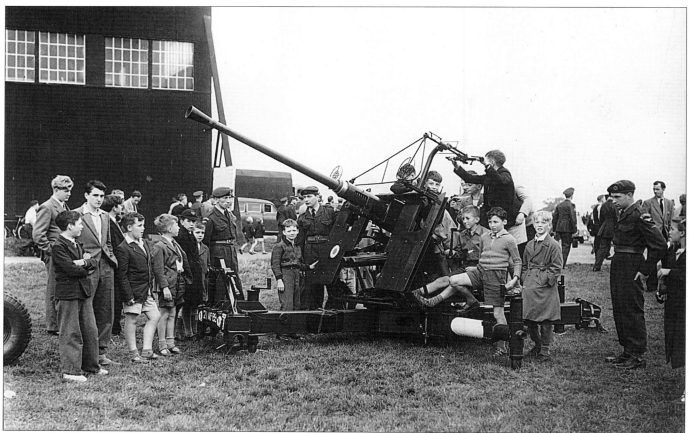

There was plenty for these youngsters to do – including manning the guns – at RAF Halton's open day in September 1950 at the end of Battle of Britain week.

An unusual combination – what in its day was one of the most modern aircraft, the Comet, and one of the oldest forms of transport, the horse and cart. They came together in June 1959 when the plane landed at RAF Halton and among those there to watch was Mr Bill Durrell, known simply as 'Uncle' and carthorse Katie. Mr Durrell worked at Halton – and so did Katie, who was believed to be the only working horse in the service of the Air Ministry!

A Vulcan jet bomber was flown in to RAF Halton in August 1964 – landing on a grass runway – to be used to help instruct the apprentices being trained there. Just in case there were any problems with the landing, a fire crew were on standby.

Banging the Drum

These five pictures show the Aylesbury branch of the Communist Party that came under attack in Market Square, Aylesbury, in June 1948 when passers-by protested against the meeting taking place in the town centre and a fight broke out.

During a pre-election campaign in 1951, the Prime Minister, Clement Attlee (previous page) visited Aylesbury and spoke in the Market Square to what appears to be a less than enthusiastic audience (above).

Prime Minister Clement Attlee seen here attending an air display at RAF Halton in 1947.

In January 1952 the Rt Hon Harold Macmillan, Minister of Housing and Local Government, visited Berryfields, Princes Risborough, to hand over the key of the 1,000th post-war 'permanent house' to be built by Wycombe Rural District Council to a Risborough ex-serviceman, his wife and two children.

Described as 'the Labour Party's prodigal son', Nye Bevan gave a speech at Aylesbury's Town Hall in May 1955.

These pictures were taken on the day in June 1955 that MP Mr G. Spencer Summers was returned to Parliament with an increased majority, He took time to meet many of those who had supported him and were waiting in the Market Square, Aylesbury to hear the result of the election count.

Important talks took place at Chequers – the country home of the Prime Minister which is close to Aylesbury – between Harold Macmillan and President Eisenhower over a weekend in September 1959. The American president acknowledged the welcoming cheers of local people as they lined the route in to Chequers, arriving in an open topped Rolls-Royce, and during his visit attended Sunday morning service at the Parish Church of St Peter and St Paul at Ellesborough.

Keen to draw attention to Conservative policies, Sir Spencer Summers – seeking to be re-elected as MP for Aylesbury – chose this rather unusual way of geting his message across during the election campaign of October 1959.

Prime Minister Harold Wilson, accompanied by his wife Mary, attending a CADRA (Cromwell Avenue and District Residents Association) fête, in Northern Road, Aylesbury.

It was in April 1948 that the Bucks and Oxford Light Infantry was granted the freedom of entry to the Borough of Aylesbury and following a march past in the Market Square the Colonel of the Regiment, General Sir Bernard Paget, took time to speak to many of those involved in the parade, in these three pictures.

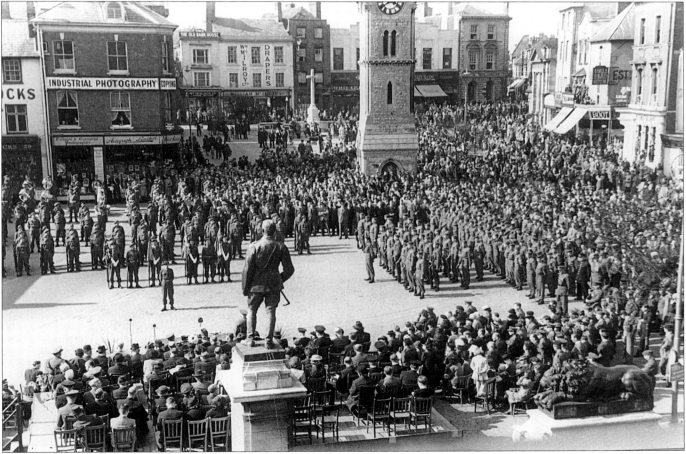

During Thanksgiving Week in October 1945, local Guides were among those to take part in a parade through Aylesbury town centre, the week of events having been officially opened by BBC announcer Mr Frederick Allen who spoke to the huge crowd from the steps of County Hall.

The following four pictures, above, next page and overleaf, show the day that RAF Halton was granted the Freedom of Aylesbury in 1956. Crowds lined the streets as the apprentices marched through the town.

The 9th Aylesbury Scouts are pictured here marching through Market Square, Aylesbury as part of the Battle of Britain Parade in September 1948.

It is an event which happens each year – Mayor's Sunday – just as it did in 1953 when the procession to St Mary's Parish Church in Aylesbury had special significance as it took place on the Sunday preceding the Coronation of Queen Elizabeth II.

Brownies are seen here marching through Aylesbury town centre in April 1958 on their way to the parish church to take part in the St George's Day service.

We Will Remember

It seems that there were few people around in the centre of Wendover in November 1949 – apart from the photographer – to watch as workmen completed the war memorial on the Manor Waste.

As the hands on the Market Square clock approach 11am, Aylesbury prepares to mark the minute of silence on Remembrance Day, 1957.

Great care was taken by craftsmen when the bronze tablets, naming Aylesbury officers and men and women who died in World War Two were placed on the war memorial in Market Square, Aylesbury in 1951.

A service of Remembrance taking place – in the road – in the village of Bishopstone in 1953.

The procession may be small in number, but the sentiments are as strong as any – Remembrance Day in Weston Turville being marked in 1953.

The Young Ones

Caught in action. Army cadets from Aylesbury on an exercise in 1947.

Special visitors to Aylesbury in February 1946 were a group of Dutch boys who spent two months in the town and, there was so much interest in their activities that they were even photographed leaving The Odeon cinema in the town!

The Whitsun weather in 1955 was not ideal for camping, but the 6th Aylesbury Scouts took the risk and headed off to Butlers Cross for a camping holiday.

The Scouts held a Jamboree and fête, in Aylesbury in July 1956. Pictured are members of the 9th Aylesbury Scouts who performed their own musical version of *Robin Hood*.

Scouts organised a pageant on the Exchange Street recreation ground in Aylesbury in July 1957.

Ready to head off to summer camp in Sussex were these Rangers just leaving the Guide Hall, Aylesbury, in 1953.

As something different for Christmas in 1958 the police and Borough Road Safety Committee arranged for Father Christmas to give away 'safety first' presents at an event in the Vale Park, Aylesbury.

Members of Weston Turville Young Farmers Club are seen here on an outing to County Farm, Stoke Mandeville in October 1957.

The choir of St Mary's Parish Church, Aylesbury, in December 1953.

Schools out! Pupils leaving Hardwick School in October 1953.

Children file into their new school in Tring Road, Aylesbury, for the first time in April 1948.

Waiting for a flight in a helicopter to have a good look at their new school are these girls who have just arrived at Hartwell House near Aylesbury in July 1957 – a finishing school for girls aged between 17 and 21 from all over the world.

Crowds watched as youngsters took part in the Queen's Park School cross country in March 1952. In the background can be seen the Molefields estate in Aylesbury which comprised pre-fabricated units housing those who had been moved to the town from other parts of the country during World War Two because of bombing.

Youngsters arriving for their first day at a new school – a completely new school! Quarrendon in Aylesbury was one of the fastest built modern schools when it opened in October 1957. Average time for building a school of this type was two years but Quarrendon, catering for 600 pupils and costing £200,000, was completed in half the time.

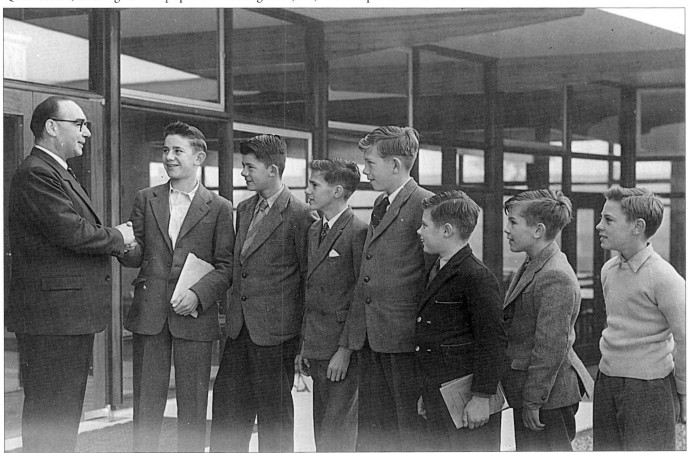

Girls on their first day at Aylesbury's new High School – the Class of '59!

St John's Church of England School in Aylesbury celebrated its 100th anniversary in July 1956 by dressing in the style of clothes which would have been worn when the school first opened and having a procession around the town.

Children with their winning garlands at May Day celebrations held at Longwick in 1953.

Infants at Wingrave school celebrating May Day in 1959 with traditional garlands of spring flowers.

Smiling youngsters from Weston Turville are pictured in 1951 helping to keep the old May Day traditions alive.